Through A Haiku Lens

Kate W. Garland

Pocahontas Press
Blacksburg, Virginia

Through A Haiku Lens

© 2015 by Kate W. Garland

All rights reserved. No part of this publication may be reproduced, stored in a retrieval system, or transmitted in any form or by any means, electronic, mechanical, photocopying, recording or otherwise, without the prior written permission of the author.

Photographs by Kate W. Garland
Photo of author by Karen E. Carlton

ISBN 10: 0-926487-56-6
ISBN 13: 9-780926-487-567
Printed in the United States of America

Published by Pocahontas Press, Blacksburg, VA
www.pocahontaspress.com

Introduction

For almost half my life, I've known how to write a haiku poem. I found the challenge to be exciting as I created a thoughtful verse, with a succinct ending, in three lines and seventeen syllables which is the traditional form of Japanese haiku. Writing haiku as a spiritual practice began when I put myself through a period of discernment with the possibility of resigning from my job and going to a place I'd never seen, a place which represented a faith practice about which I knew very little. The decision to go would mean leaving Maine to attend a winter semester student program at Pendle Hill Quaker Study Center in Wallingford, Pennsylvania, in 2001. Forgoing the security of a job, not knowing if there would be the possibility of employment for me when I came back after three-and-a-half months away, was daunting. At the age of almost 65, I was not in high demand for employment, especially since I'd spent most of the decade of the 1990s as a volunteer in various religious retreat/conference centres, and one church, in Scotland. In the midst of my agonizing deliberations, an almost fully-intact haiku came into my head, and I confidently made the decision. To quote the poet Robert Frost, I entered the road less traveled "and that has made all the difference."

> **bird knows when to fly**
> **depart the place of refuge**
> **trusting wing and wind**

At the end of the semester at Pendle Hill, I was offered an opportunity to attend, tuition free, the spring semester. A student intern was leaving at the end of the winter semester, and I could take her place in fulfilling her year-long commitment. It was tempting. I decided to stay. Taking a short break, I went back to Maine, retrieved my car and drove to Pendle Hill before beginning the semester. Toward the end of the spring semester, I was offered a summer paid job of housekeeping and hospitality. I accepted. Not wanting to continue paying rent on an apartment I hadn't lived in since December, 2000, I submitted my 30-day notice of termination to the landlord. Another trip to Maine. I hurriedly packed my possessions, put them in storage, and once again returned to Pendle Hill before the summer work began. In August, I was offered a full-time job as hospitality coordinator which I accepted without any doubts. By then, I knew I was not going back to Maine as a state resident any time in the near future. Once again to Maine, but this time to rent a U-Haul truck to transport my goods from the storage unit to Portland, Maine. A friend and I then transferred all my goods to an ABC truck so that a driver could transport my belongings to a storage unit in Pennsylvania. I was now ready to begin my newest adventure and challenge of living and working in another religious community, this time in the U.S.A.

I was committed both to living at Pendle Hill and to the faith practice of the Quakers, The Religious Society of Friends. My place of work and worship became a modern monastic oasis for me. My creative nature thrived; the haiku flowed out of my mind and heart. Haiku has been a constant creative endeavor during all the years I lived and worked in Scotland from 1993 to 1999; Orono, Maine, from 1999 to 2001; Pendle Hill, from January, 2001 to July, 2003; Floyd, Virginia, from 2003 to 2012, and now as I live in Blacksburg, Virginia. The poetry is predominately about the natural world wherever I lived at any given time. In traditional Japanese haiku, nature, seasons, time and place in the present moment are common themes. Other themes in the haiku I've written through the years are about my relationship with the people and also the work/social environments. When I read some of the haiku I've written, I often can recall vividly in my mind's eye the circumstances in the moment of the experience.

I now live in a planned community of people, mostly over 50 years of age, in Blacksburg, Virginia. Haiku continues to interpret my life and surroundings in a way that brings clarity to my understanding. The haiku I write now often emerge from my experiences of aging and through the wonders of nature surrounding me, with the change of seasons stimulating my creative juices. I find that the past holds treasures of experiences and insights for me to glean for my poetry. Using a traditional haiku form with a 20th, now 21st century mind-set, my poetry is like a journal of my thoughts, feelings, longings, contradictions, and observations. In the case of my sometimes off-beat sense of humor, the haiku can make sense in a rather distorted way or it enters the realm of nonsense.

through a haiku lens
clarity of mind and heart
bursts with purity

The book has been arranged so that the left side of each open page is blank. I invite you to use those blank pages as a journal to record a memory or feeling that a poem may evoke. You may try creating your own poetry or drawing an illustration that has meaning for you. Please, however, don't alter the poems I have written – they are uniquely mine. This book of haiku represents word-pictures from my life journey. Let your own incomparable life be a catalyst for you to be creative.

Acknowledgements

The first twenty-two years of my life were lived in Ames, Iowa. Through childhood and into young adulthood, I experienced the changes of seasons, the expansive quality of the land, the vibrancy of the natural world, the sense of neighborhood where my family lived, and the Mid-western integrity of the people in my family's orbit. All this shaped my imagination and my awareness of how important place and people are in contributing to my well-being, no matter where I live. My brother, sister-in-law, a nephew and his family still live in Iowa and periodically I need to reclaim my roots as I return to visit family and attend my high school reunions. I am humbly grateful that my now deceased parents, Elizabeth and Wallace Wright, Sr., chose to live and raise their family in Iowa.

I'm grateful to a now ex-husband for introducing me to the Japanese poetry form of haiku as it seems to fit my tendency for conciseness in my creative efforts. My first major curriculum at Iowa State College (now University) was Applied Art, and I still have a charcoal drawing I did of a grain silo beside a railroad track which bordered the college. The students in the class were told to go out on the campus and do sketches of the buildings and grounds. My sketch certainly didn't resemble those of any other artist as their sketches were filled with details and shadings. My work was stark, filled with a sense of isolation. Detail was not a part of my artistic interest or vocabulary, so I decided not to pursue art as a potential profession any longer. It's been quite revealing to me that the spare quality of my visual art is now apparent in the brevity of my chosen form of poetry as I challenge myself, and anyone who reads my haiku, to experience the essence and depth of what the very short haiku poem can offer. I realize now that creating visual art was not my passion, but it is the poetry form of haiku that excites and challenges me. It requires a focus that eliminates extraneous description.

In presenting this assortment of poems, I decided to organize them into sections and was able to identify five themes as appropriate. However, I discovered that haiku poems are a lot like cats, who can present different persona within any given day or season of the year. Therefore, you may find that a poem in The Nature of Nature could also be suitable in Time and Place. I just decided "so be it," and I'd trust the reader to ponder whether I sensed the appropriate place for those ambiguous poems.

I'm indebted to many people who have read the haiku I've written, offering comments and encouragement about how the poems stirred some emotional or intellectual response in them. Some people have let me know how, in their consideration, a poem may fail to deliver the startling conclusive word or phrase that is needed. There are also people who respond with an impulsive "ahh," "yes," laughter or thoughtful silence followed by affirmations of an emotional or visceral effect of a poem after hearing me read.

With reluctance that I may not remember all the people who have read and responded to my haiku and who have read some of my other writing efforts through the years, I'll try to acknowledge those in my memory who have been instrumental in supporting me in my work as a poet and published author. My apology to anyone whose name I've failed to record here. Please know you have been a contributing part of my almost forty years of writing haiku and other literary forms of fantasy and reality. I offer grateful appreciation to Karen, Patricia A., Arthur, Dennis R., Sheena, Jean, Douglas, Yvonne, Connie, Irene, Jennifer M., Mary S., Lee, Tom, Dennis N., Patricia M., Margaret, Janeal, Charlie, Ella, Joyce A., Mary Stuart C., and all others who have been exposed to my pen-to-paper, fingers-to-keyboard outpourings. Also, special thanks to my publisher, Jane, for her guidance in bringing my writings to book form and to her editorial staff.

Dedication

This book is dedicated to John and Andrew, who make the world a better place with their integrity, intelligence, and quick witted sense of humor. I love you dearly.

The Nature of Nature

a weathered tree stump
becomes a garden with the
help of a gardener

Through A Haiku Lens

Kate W. Garland

                    under a sun drenched
                    sky – acres of colorful
                      tulips in full bloom

suddenly bare trees
seem laced with edges of green
spring softens winter

Through A Haiku Lens

Kate W. Garland

vibrant crocus buds
resting in beds of white snow
season confusion

bare branch in winter
decorated only by
a red feathered bird

Through A Haiku Lens

Kate W. Garland

                    two spiders on one
         slender silk web – like swordsmen
                they parry and thrust

caught in the middle
squirrel zigs and zags before
its bloody demise

Through A Haiku Lens

Kate W. Garland

                                                rain drop glistening
                                  quivering on soft green leaf
                                                    new day beginning

day awakes to life
sun obscured by heavy clouds
day comes anyway

Through A Haiku Lens

Kate W. Garland

                                          mountain wildflower
                          growing from beneath the rock
                                              she seeks the sunlight

tree firmly grounded
reaching deeply into earth
where roots are nourished

Through A Haiku Lens

Kate W. Garland

> winter turns to spring
> and green shoots of life appear
> where snow has melted

lovely marigolds
bright yellow petals bloom in
clay pots on my deck

Through A Haiku Lens

Kate W. Garland

             bees tease the clover
       drinking deeply the goodness
              in the small flower

drifting in the wind
leaf skittles like a dancer
for my amusement

Through A Haiku Lens

Kate W. Garland

                    wind disturbs the leaf
          red-bronzed glory fades to brown
                and leaf floats to earth

willow tree branches
bend and swing in response to
wind's wild forcefulness

Through A Haiku Lens

Kate W. Garland

>wild raging waters
>strong resistant ancient rocks
>meet with brutal force
>*Isle of Mull, Scotland – 1993*

gathering blue-gray
clouds against evergreen and
pine before a storm

Through A Haiku Lens

Kate W. Garland

>willow branches sway
in the breeze as though they are
playing together

breezes gently stir
yellow daffodils after
a soft spring rainfall

Through A Haiku Lens

Kate W. Garland

> two birds rest on stones
> within the wall encircling
> the silent graveyard

bird is motionless
it seems to sense something I
don't hear or detect

Through A Haiku Lens

Kate W. Garland

> water cascading
> over rugged rocks falls to
> troubled pool below

water curls into
water - rising in white spray
before descending

Through A Haiku Lens

Kate W. Garland

                                          tail curled over back
                                  squirrel nibbles hurriedly
                                              eyes furtively dart

spider approaches
as I sit on the park bench
silent intrusion

Through A Haiku Lens

Kate W. Garland

                                        sky blue day to lift
                                    my spirit after endless
                                    shrouding winter gray

first purple blossom
of tiny crocus revives
my sagging spirit

Through A Haiku Lens

Kate W. Garland

                                            wild goose flies beyond
                                            limits of endurance - she
                                              knows no other way

an inner knowing
not reason or thought as bird
suddenly takes flight

Through A Haiku Lens

Kate W. Garland

                                      field of wildflowers
                            scattered like colorful gems
                                          on a vast green rug

rainbow appearing
with its broad arc of color
after a rainstorm

Through A Haiku Lens

Kate W. Garland

                                                dewdrop glistening
                                       in the morning sun offers
                                                   prism perfection

snow on snow on snow
winter blizzards' aftermath
white serenity

Through A Haiku Lens

Kate W. Garland

                                        strength and fruitfulness
                                          is the character of a
                                              tree firmly rooted

lilacs bloom on bush
awakening from winter's
paralyzing grip

Through A Haiku Lens

Kate W. Garland

                                        creatures seek comfort
                               as nights become colder and
                                    chill winds disturb sleep

wind blows where it will
turning umbrellas inside
out – roiling the sea

Through A Haiku Lens

Kate W. Garland

                      squirrel is airborne
            flying from tree branch to branch
                        someday it will fall

wind rustling brilliant
yellow leaves not yet fallen
an autumn ritual

Through A Haiku Lens

Kate W. Garland

                      bark looking grizzled
              and gray – protecting the life
                        that lies beneath it

tiny wildflowers
in unexpected places
easily ignored

Through A Haiku Lens

The Human Condition

lord of the manor
sipping tea from a thermos
cup – all's well today

Through A Haiku Lens

Kate W. Garland

> girl with a sunshine
> smile like solar energy
> it radiates warmth

young warriors on the
playing field with one desire
to defeat the foe

Through A Haiku Lens

Kate W. Garland

when I am old I
will exercise using a
purple yoga mat

in years I'm old - in
spirit I'm ageless - spirit
knows best who I am

Through A Haiku Lens

Kate W. Garland

>
> winter leaves no place
> for my soul to take refuge
> except inwardly

noises swirl around
me as I sit in silent
centered contentment

Through A Haiku Lens

Kate W. Garland

nursery school nearly
warped my spirit – thankfully
I didn't let it

I'm not the brightest
penny in the purse but I
do add some value

Through A Haiku Lens

Kate W. Garland

                                            beloved you are
                              beyond my reach as we live
                                      in two different worlds

letting go is a
lesson in learning how to
grow old joyfully

Through A Haiku Lens

Kate W. Garland

> I am a restless
> pilgrim eager to walk new
> roads awaiting me

may you defy all
expectations and live at
the critical edge

Through A Haiku Lens

Kate W. Garland

                        dreary Monday slows
                      me in preparations to
                            be responsible

malaise seeps into
my consciousness like a mist
of mind numbing gloom

Through A Haiku Lens

Kate W. Garland

                                  gentle rain streaming
                    down your upturned face as you
                          spoke of truth and love

beautiful embers
of friendship after wild flames
that passion began

Through A Haiku Lens

Kate W. Garland

                              images of love
              the young full and ripe with lust
                         tenderly the old

moving slowly two
old friends preparing their tea
not many secrets

Through A Haiku Lens

Kate W. Garland

                        take away my hair
           add wrinkles, aches, hampered sight
                  but my smile won't dim

dance in the moonlight
or under the sun – just dance
to your soul's heartbeat

Through A Haiku Lens

Kate W. Garland

　　　　　　　　　　　I'm on a high speed
　　　　　　　　　　carousel – wind in my hair
　　　　　　　　　　we're going somewhere

Little Dictator
in my head won't let me drift
like ancient flotsam

Through A Haiku Lens

Kate W. Garland

> I mourn the loss of
> my youth and relish the rich
> insights of aging

woman of shadows
allows sun's light to reach her
so reluctantly

Through A Haiku Lens

Kate W. Garland

goodness is in the
world – pulsating from hearts and
minds of pure intent

mother's milk flowing
river of life giving life
strengthening the weak

Through A Haiku Lens

Kate W. Garland

                                        attracts and repels
                              by his actions – a fractured
                                    wounded loving soul

through a dark tunnel
where hope disappears or light
dispels the despair

Through A Haiku Lens

Kate W. Garland

                                            as a snake sheds skin
                                        so I grow from center out
                                            bursting confinement

children and adults
equally enthralled by the
young poet's passion
Rainy day - St. Oswald's Church
Grassmere, England 19 September 2011

Through A Haiku Lens

Kate W. Garland

					sometimes I feel odd
				and out of place in this world
						of technology

I know earthly life
is mortal but death took my
cherished friend too soon

Through A Haiku Lens

Kate W. Garland

> I live on the verge
> of creativity or
> chaos - which is it

grandparents have the
responsibility of
knowing how to play

Through A Haiku Lens

Kate W. Garland

                                                            mother died – it was
                                                           April and very sudden
                                                          next day soft snow fell

his smile was brilliant
not a handsome little guy
but he touched my heart

Through A Haiku Lens

Time and Place

snack shack for hungry
hikers and all others who
simply love the place

Through A Haiku Lens

Kate W. Garland

                                        what do I treasure
                                 peace harmony belonging
                                     a place I call home

cat's feet walk softly
confident her demeanor
she knows the way home

Through A Haiku Lens

Kate W. Garland

                                                  sun hides behind trees
                                        seems to be dropping to earth
                                            before night enshrouds

water-colored sky
sinks into languid landscape
bird glides easily

Through A Haiku Lens

Kate W. Garland

                                                                    two champagne glasses
                                                                     10 a.m. train to Scotland
                                                                          economy coach

slow bus to city
of Edinburgh – my day
off – I breathe deeply

Through A Haiku Lens

Kate W. Garland

                                        cat's imperious
                            eye warns against disrupting
                                her while eating lunch

with eyes to see and
ears to hear perceptive cat
stares with intention

Through A Haiku Lens

Kate W. Garland

                    wood-smoke scented wind
                rich memories beyond warmth
                        for body and soul

wood-smoke scented wind
cleansing and purifying
smudging my spirit

Through A Haiku Lens

Kate W. Garland

                          tulips in cluster
            surround the sturdy tree trunk
                       a proud color guard

gentle blossom grows
among thorns and cruel winds
her beauty shining

Through A Haiku Lens

Kate W. Garland

                                        water filled pot sinks
                                        washers waiting to begin
                                        hands their tools of work

squirrel in dumpster
unaware of each other
I empty my trash

Through A Haiku Lens

Kate W. Garland

spring breezes dancing
through open doors and windows
soft undulations

luminous moonlight
dancing over dark water
like sparkling gemstones

Through A Haiku Lens

Kate W. Garland

                                                  cool chill of autumn
                                     is great relief from summer's
                                                      brash intensity

cold damp morning air
curl into myself for warmth
time can wait for me

Through A Haiku Lens

Kate W. Garland

                                                               trusting someone to
                                                              arrive as expected – a
                                                                    fragile agreement

stepping stones offer
a way forward as I trust
their strength and support

Through A Haiku Lens

Kate W. Garland

             cat licking her paw
             ignoring all around her
             or so it would seem

birds articulate
filling the air with sounds of
life in the moment

Through A Haiku Lens

Kate W. Garland

> Karen's new home is
> a Light/light place where her soul
> and spirit will thrive

cat disregards space
assumes the right to come close
she knows what she needs

Through A Haiku Lens

Kate W. Garland

                    gusting winds and rain
           obscure the Quiraing from sight
                      I know it's still there
                Isle of Skye, Scotland - 1998

rugged hills marked with
gray rocks and carpets of green
softened by heather

Through A Haiku Lens

Kate W. Garland

                                  I walk country roads
                    fields of green corn on both sides
                                      becoming mature

for whom the bell tolls
tells me to pause and listen
to my heart beating

Through A Haiku Lens

Kate W. Garland

                                                    wild Maine blueberries
                                                    tiny fragrant summer fruit
                                                        make good winter pies

winter is a gift
of grace as my spirit moves
inward and snow falls

Through A Haiku Lens

Kate W. Garland

                    red bird looking for
            food on my deck nourishing
                        me by its presence

fire of light and warmth
burn, consume the wood and air
end of camper's day

Through A Haiku Lens

Kate W. Garland

                                            she is a special
                            cat who understands that time's
                                               a fluid concept

a scent of autumn
in the midst of summer and
nights become cooler

Through A Haiku Lens

Kate W. Garland

                        like sparkling jewels
            scattered over black velvet
                Glasgow from the sky
                  First trip to Scotland
                      19 December 1991

country dancing in
the village hall after a
few pints in the pub
Isle of Iona, Scotland

Through A Haiku Lens

Sense and Nonsense

I Lily can be
anything – a vulture or
a watch cat on guard

Through A Haiku Lens

Kate W. Garland

> God in the because
> beyond our reasoning minds
> into no-sense sense

sometimes change is wise
as a necessary act
of re-creation

Through A Haiku Lens

Kate W. Garland

                                      as I try to make
                    sense of my life the cat yawns
                         and closes her eyes

the cat smiled at me
yes he did I know he did
so I smiled at him

Through A Haiku Lens

Kate W. Garland

                    summer slowly crawls
            t'ward cooler days when autumn
                flaunts her brilliant hues

she floats on her back —
summer requires a slower
mode for peace of mind

Through A Haiku Lens

Kate W. Garland

                                                edges fit neatly
                                  and tightly together when
                                          fashioned carefully

letters I never
wrote – words I never spoke – what
did I lose or gain

Through A Haiku Lens

Kate W. Garland

                    light notes fly from flute
                    into air as muses waltz
                        joyfully on clouds

three muses look down
on me with jealous glances
as I sip coffee
A painting in Natasha's Market Café
 & Gallery - Floyd, VA

Through A Haiku Lens

Kate W. Garland

                        sun rise then sun set
                      an improbable quandary
                     earth moves sun does not

when desire calls me
beyond time and space will I
go with grateful heart

Through A Haiku Lens

Kate W. Garland

                                                  we've lost our sense of
                                                  subtleties seeing life in
                                                      magic marker hues

my left eye making
unreasonable demands quite
like my ego I

Through A Haiku Lens

Kate W. Garland

                                          Late instead of Kate
                                      an error or computer
                                          exposing my faults

to Mercy Mary
reliable companion
your cause of death – rust

Through A Haiku Lens

Kate W. Garland

                                          manipulating
                       Marla plays by her own rules
                        when she wants something

Maricella the
drama queen leaves vivid hues
swirling in her wake

Through A Haiku Lens

Kate W. Garland

                                          Daphne looked lovely
                                   at her high school reunion
                                              she enjoyed herself

Daisy Mae delight-
ful child of wisdom and joy
but mostly of play

Through A Haiku Lens

Kate W. Garland

                                        Tizzie McGee seems
                                  always to land on her feet
                                sometimes in whipped cream

Ukiah Haiku
wears his clothes inside out and
eats his dessert first

Through A Haiku Lens

The Sacred and the Ordinary

the sacred and the
ordinary are present
in each breath I take

Through A Haiku Lens

Kate W. Garland

                                                    Abbey ghost winds sing
                                   ancient voices join with ours
                                                       worshipping as one
                                     Isle of Iona, Scotland – 1993

my heart breaks with joy
among trees and living stones
of still Columcille
Megalith Park - Bangor, PA

Through A Haiku Lens

Kate W. Garland

                small box of cheese chunks
              and digestive biscuits - soul
                  food from a soul friend

French lentil soup and
focaccia bread nourishing
one's body and soul

Through A Haiku Lens

Kate W. Garland

                                        a power beyond
                            the reasoning mind is our
                                              imagination

through a mystic lens
clarity beyond my sight
altered perception

Through A Haiku Lens

Kate W. Garland

                    we are embraced in
                    the radiant mystery
                    of God's light and love

I am a child of
God whose inward light and love
radiate my life

Through A Haiku Lens

Kate W. Garland

                    yesterday's routines
              don't work anymore – today
                      I must reassess

the matter is clear
the superficial must go
for simplicity

Through A Haiku Lens

Kate W. Garland

                    simple meal between
            two friends becomes a ritual
                 of shared communion

laughter is delight
when shared with a beloved
unreservedly

Through A Haiku Lens

Kate W. Garland

>
> Jesus is being
> Spirit breathes into your soul
> I am what I am

impulse of God sends
radiating energy
through ordered cosmos

Through A Haiku Lens

Kate W. Garland

>
> small candles glowing
> sending tiny rays of light
> to join the darkness

clouds obscure the sun
like a truth waiting to be
revealed in its time

Through A Haiku Lens

Kate W. Garland

> rest in God whose warm
> embrace is love unearned and
> unconditional

love is stronger than
fear or anger or all claims
that hold us captive

Through A Haiku Lens

Kate W. Garland

                                          Christmas approaching
                          who would know amid the blitz
                                              of frenzied shopping

gratitude bursts with
charity through the ramparts
of my resistance

Through A Haiku Lens

Kate W. Garland

                                                       at the still center
                                        where emptiness exists is
                                            the wellspring of life

centered in spirit
Felicity walks the earth
she is who she is

Through A Haiku Lens

Kate W. Garland

                                        stepping stones, fragile
                  dreams and twilight zones transport
                                              me into beyond

black birds, eagles, white
clouds weave a mystical dance
for my upturned eyes

Through A Haiku Lens

Kate W. Garland

                      seeking contentment
                  I find disturbance until
                        lightening my load

give thanks and be glad
each dawn is a renewal
of hope and promise

Through A Haiku Lens

Kate W. Garland

                                              dwelling within us
                                          is a presence of divine
                                            providence and love

let love grow in your
heart infusing the world with
a gentle spirit

Through A Haiku Lens

Kate W. Garland

through dark wilderness
with hope often dashed and bruised
the way is still clear

healing hope brings calm
when in the midst of chaos
restoring balance

Through A Haiku Lens

Kate W. Garland

                         butterfly wings seem
                    fragile until reaching out
                       in flight and new life

divine grace changes
my clouded mind to accept
beauty as it is

Through A Haiku Lens

Kate W. Garland

                                    pray for reasoned calm
                        may the bird of peace find home
                             through gathering storm

peace cannot happen
when hearts and minds are closed to
the impulse of love

Through A Haiku Lens

Kate W. Garland

        silence informs me
bringing a new awareness
       to mind and spirit

silence in worship
with others is communion
of souls and Spirit
Unprogrammed Quaker worship

www.ingramcontent.com/pod-product-compliance
Lightning Source LLC
Chambersburg PA
CBHW050637300426
44112CB00012B/1832